PRIVATE EYE

Colemanballs

13

A selection of quotes,
most of which originally appeared
in PRIVATE EYE's
'Colemanballs' column.

Our thanks once again to all the readers
who sent us their contributions,
and to whom this book is dedicated.

PRIVATE EYE
Colemanballs
13

Compiled and edited by
BARRY FANTONI

Illustrated by Tony Husband

PRIVATE EYE

Published in Great Britain
by Private Eye Productions Ltd,
6 Carlisle Street, London W1D 3BN

© 2006 Pressdram Ltd
ISBN 1 901784 45 2
Designed by Bridget Tisdall
Printed in Great Britain by
Clays Ltd, St Ives plc

Athletics

"The British team will need to pull their socks out."

STEVE CRAM

"This is the time when your team manager is worth more than salt."

COLIN JACKSON

"And here's Moses Kiptanui, the 19-year-old Kenyan who turned 20 a few weeks ago."

DAVID COLEMAN

"This would be the cream on the jam for her..."

STUART STOREY

"She [Paula Radcliffe] has thrown all her eggs mentally into the marathon basket."

GRAHAM BEECROFT

"The women triathlon athletes have had their numbers branded on."

RADIO 5 LIVE

"I came fifth in Helsinki, which is gold if you remove all the American and non-European athletes."

TIM BENJAMIN

"There is only one word for it: it's got to be a foul."

BRENDAN FOSTER

"Paula Radcliffe has been absolutely castrated by the media."

RADIO 5 LIVE

"So for Linford Christie to get the job he'll have to prove whiter than white..."

VICTORIA DERBYSHIRE

Boxing

"Genetically, [Amir] Khan looks a lot bigger than [Daniel] Thorpe."

DUKE McKENZIE

"Suddenly it became a one-horse fight."

STEVE BUNCE

Cans

"He is, unfortunately, just the tip of the iceberg and this has opened a can of worms."

SUSAN MOORE

"In a way I became the can of worms because I opened it and they exploded."

YOLANDE BECKLES

"Shane Warne turned around like a can of beans."

MICHAEL ATHERTON

Cricket

"There's always pressure – we just need to stick to our toes."

KEVIN PIETERSEN

"I hope these young West Indian players do realise the mantle on which they are standing."

VIV RICHARDS

"... that shot was as straight as a whistle."

TONY GREIG

"He [Graham Thorpe] is a good footballer so he has that instinctive hand-eye coordination."

MICHAEL ATHERTON

"He knows his limitations and he just sticks to them."

MIKE GATTING

"Marcus Trescothick celebrates his one hundredth hundred with a century."

RUSSELL FULLER

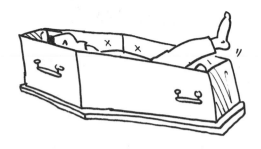

"Harmison posthumously puts out a foot..."
RADIO 4

"They need to bowl one ball at a time."
IAN BISHOP

"This is a viper's nest waiting to be unfurled..."
JONATHAN AGNEW

"He's been given an opportunity to play Test Cricket and he's taken it with both feet."
DOMINIC CORK

"There is no player alive today, with the exception of Don Bradman, who hasn't gone through a bad patch."
MICHAEL ATHERTON

"Keepers normally go for the ball with two hands, and then when it looks like getting out of reach, the other one comes into play."

TONY GREIG

"In this series, a lot of them [England batsmen] have made the wrong mistakes."

GEOFFREY BOYCOTT

"It defied gravity and dropped like a stone..."

SKY SPORTS

"South Africa won't just lie back and let the last rites be thrown down at them."

ALLEN DONALD

"Pietersen is jumping about like a cat on hot tin bricks."

CHRISTOPHER MARTIN-JENKINS

"You couldn't have placed that any better – talk about a needle in a haystack."

IAN BOTHAM

"He [Andrew Flintoff] is going nine to the dozen."

RAY PRICE

"He's got to do it mentally, without thinking about it."

GEOFFREY BOYCOTT

"He [Graeme Smith] is capable of reading other people's heads."

NASSER HUSSAIN

"That's putting the horse in the stable after it's left."

GEOFF BOYCOTT

"Here at Lord's, it's lovely blue sunshine."

HENRY BLOFELD

"Winning the Ashes was not the peak for us; it was another notch on the ladder we're climbing up."
MARCUS TRESCOTHICK

"He is bowling on that good length just short of a good length."
PAUL ALLOTT

"I'm not too sure if we can [regain the Ashes], but I'm sure we will do."
MICHAEL VAUGHAN

"We'll *all* be the first to hold up our hands and take it on the chin."
ASHLEY GILES

"When he's on fire, he's hot."
BILL LAWRY

"Harmison would have been out if the ball had hit the stumps."
MARK NICHOLAS

"He's not a hooker, but he's a worker of the ball."

GEOFFREY BOYCOTT

"He's played the shot of the day twice now."

GRAEME FOWLER

"Two wins will give them a great fillip to their cap..."

GRAHAM GOOCH

"Well, the proof of the pudding is at the end of the day."

GEOFFREY BOYCOTT

"They [New Zealand] were caught between two limbos."

MIKE GATTING

"Here comes Shabir Ahmed. He's not as young as most Pakistanis. He's 27."

CHRISTOPHER MARTIN-JENKINS

"His arms were too far away from his body."

GEOFFREY BOYCOTT

"He [Matthew Hayden] is an attractive man, and so is his wife."

SARAH KENNEDY

"Of course he [Michael Vaughan] should be at the birth of his first child – it's something he'll only experience 2, 3 or maybe 4 times in his life."

STEPHEN BRIERLY

"I've just turned 36. The likelihood is in four years' time I'll be 40."

SHANE WARNE

"Harper there, the massive umpire from Australia, arms folded behind his backs."

HENRY BLOFELD

Cycling

"The riders have come back from the face of adversary."

PHIL LIGGETT

Darts

"He has a chance this afternoon to put history into the past."

TONY GREEN

"A game of darts is a game of darts and you've got to play the player you're playing."

ANDY FORDHAM

"Clean as a whistle and as fast..."

TONY GREEN

Football

"England have the best fans in the world and Scotland's fans are second to none."

KEVIN KEEGAN

"Larry [Simon Grayson] did well in midfield today, but we do need someone in there with more legs."

COLIN HENDRY

"Roy Keane going to Celtic would be a case of out of the goldfish bowl, into the fire."

CATHAL DERVAN

"Meanwhile, it's Birmingham nil, Spurs nil: that one will be kicking off in a couple of hours."

TALK SPORT RADIO

"He [Alan Shearer] is arguably the best footballer this country has ever produced. I don't think anyone can argue with that."

DANNY HIGGINBOTHAM

"When it doesn't rain, it pours."

COLIN COOPER

"He's a big king in a small pool."

ALAN GREEN

"A home win could have been a milestone around our necks, but now we've put it to bed."

ALAN PARDEW

"Every Celtic player will wear the number seven jersey on his shorts."

MURDO MacLEOD

"For all their possession, Preston have only had one shot on target, and that was off target."

JOHN PEARSON

"He's just thrown his head in there and it's just come off."

JOHN DUNCAN

"Glen Roeder will think for a few minutes before making a rash decision."

STEVE STONE

"Sven should be hauled before the coals..."

GRAHAM BEECROFT

"A better statistician than me will tell you that he [Reyes] has scored once every 58 minutes he has been on the pitch this season."

JOHN MOTSON

"Their goal on the stroke of half-time unsettled us, and, no matter what you say during the interval, there's that little bit of toothache in their minds."

STEVE COPPELL

"Let me throw something into the boiling point here..."

RAY STUBBS

"It was still a shock when George died. It was the last thing I thought he'd do."

ANGIE BEST

"It was like they had lost a limb because he [Eric Cantona] was the backbone of that side."

EDITH BOWMAN

"There is only one word to describe football and that is 'if only'."

BOBBY ROBSON

"He favours his left-hand foot..."

CHRIS WADDLE

"Joe Cole had a slash on the edge of the box and it actually found its way back to the corner flag."

COLIN COOPER

"Five minutes to go and England have a winning lead..."

JOHN MOTSON

"And, in case you're wondering, Jagielka is related to his younger brother at Sheffield United, Phil."

KEVIN KEATINGS

"The Watford fans have thrown graffiti on the pitch."

RADIO 5 LIVE

"How things have changed [at Torquay United] in the last two years. Mike Bateson was the chairman then... and he's still the chairman now."

HAMISH MARSHALL

"There are a lot of tired legs wearing Tottenham shirts."

ANDY GRAY

"Fulham needed those three points because they were slowly sinking towards the bottom very very quickly."

MARK LAWRENSON

"You have to score goals these days to win international matches."

JIMMY ARMFIELD

"He [Dunfermline Athletic chairman John Yorkston] just pulled the rugs out from under the players' carpets."

ANDY WALKER

"Arsene Wenger has just hitched up his trousers. He's a very relieved man indeed."

SKY

"Souness has got rid of his coat and is just in his jacket sleeves."

JOHN MURRAY

"He's always been an excellent dribbler, both with and without the ball."

TALKSPORT

"[The pitch is] as flat as a dodo."

DAVID LLOYD

"They've [Rosenberg] had a holocaust of a start..."

TERRY VENABLES

"He's got a great right foot, and if he can get his head around that he'll be a great player."

RAY WILKINS

"I can look in the mirror every day and be pleased with what I'm doing, never rattling anyone's feathers."

MICHAEL OWEN

"I don't think players care too much about stats and statistics…"

ASHLEY COLE

"I can assure West Ham fans that no stone will be unearthed in our preparation for next week."

ALAN PARDEW

"The only way I can spend is to buy."

KEVIN KEEGAN

"They [Everton FC] are really missing the loss of Arteta. It's sticking out like a sore throat."

RONNIE GOODLASS

"This is a Cup Final in its own right."

JOHN MOTSON

"I want to finish as high as we can, and I think that's possible."

DAVID O'LEARY

"I don't want to sound homophobic, but I want a Scottish manager."

PAT NEVIN

"If Everton finish in a Champions League place, they'll play in the Champions League."

MARK BRIGHT

"They [Arsenal] have to concentrate not only when they have the ball or when their opponents have the ball, but also when neither of them has the ball."

RADIO 5 LIVE

"So, this movie you star in, The Life Story of George Best – tell us, what is it about?"

GEORGE GAVIN

"There's no magic formula that says A plus C equals X."

TERRY VENABLES

"The clock seems to be moving quicker. For the first time, the sight is in end."

DAVID PLEAT

"Sheffield Wednesday have put the cat amongst the bag."

REPORTER, BBC1

"Keith Gillespie... just lacks a bit of inconsistency."
GRAEME LE SAUX

"Yes, Robbie Savage's a lovely feller, but when he's on the pitch he holds no bars..."
GARY SPEED

"He [Souness] has just gone behind my back in front of my face."
CRAIG BELLAMY

"This half Liverpool are attacking their fans, who are packed into the away end."
RADIO 5 LIVE

"It's Oliver Kahn's turn to taste the ball in the back of the goal."

ANDY TOWNSEND

"He [Ken Bates] has never been afraid to shirk any responsibilities."

NORMAN HUNTER

"Manchester United is a huge hurdle and we are keeping our feet on the ground."

IAN HUXHAM

"Sunderland, making a rare soirée into Wolves' territory..."

SIMON CRABTREE

"Ian Dowie knows that any points dropped at home are points dropped."

JASON CUNDY

"You want to be on the winning side – and if you are, you're the winner."

GRAHAM TAYLOR

"All the other speculation is pure speculation."

ALAN CURBISHLEY

"Retiring will put years on his career."

DON HOWE

"I don't know where this Arctic wind has come from, but it's freezing."

ALAN GREEN

"Sunderland are breathing down the shorts of Wigan."

MARK BRIGHT

"If Oldham are going to get anything out of this game, they've got a battle to climb."

RADIO 5 LIVE

"There's a whole lot of teams in the bottom six."
GRAEME LE SAUX

"He [Roy Keane] showed a total lack of disrespect."
JEFF WINTER

"Novo did well to get his body between himself and the ball."
JIM DUFFY

"You don't want Rooney to come in your box."
GRAEME LE SAUX

"There are big and there are big games. This is the latter."
BBC RADIO BRISTOL

"He's a bit like a puppeteer because he's playing us all like fiddles."
RAY STUBBS

"Lampard put his shot in the bottom-hand corner."
GLENN HODDLE

"I thought we started very, very brightly but then the Achilles Heel which has bitten us in the backside all year has stood out like a sore thumb."

ANDY KING

" 'Que sera sera' they chanted in English."

HENRY WINTER

"Jose Mourinho has got the Midas touch right now – everything he touches turns to silver."

RICHARD KEYES

"In this day and age you don't see too many footballers with two feet."

PETER ALLEN

"Football has got a nasty habit of biting you straight in the face."

CHARLIE NICHOLLS

"When you make a mistake, that becomes a mistake."

TERRY VENABLES

"Wales clinging on to a foothold..."

JOHN MOTSON

"Arsene Wenger's lips are firmly sealed on Sir Alex Ferguson."

CHRIS SKUDDER

"The offside flag went up immediately if not before."

JONATHAN PARK

"For midfielders, it's very difficult to score without the ball."

RODNEY MARSH

"They [Aston Villa] seem to beat the teams halfway down but struggle against the teams halfway up."

MARK LAWRENSON

"... they [Newcastle FC supporters] see Owen as some kind of Masonic personality."

RADIO 5 LIVE

"He [Glen Johnson] is breathing pretty hard, but I suppose that's his own way of getting air into his lungs."

JIM NEILLY

"It was the centenary event to mark twenty-five years since we won the cup."

TREVOR FRANCIS

"We've got the quality to beat them but we haven't."

IAN WRIGHT

"I don't think that Sven Goran Eriksson's command of the English language is as good as what you'd like it to be."

TREVOR FRANCIS

"The only bad thing about our situation is the situation itself."

GARY MEGSON

"The game is in a neutral country, for both teams."

DAVID BECKHAM

"And that was Stelios! Or – to give him his full name – Giannakopoulos of Bolton."

JOHN MOTSON

"Wayne [Rooney] likes to play in the little hole behind me."

MICHAEL OWEN

"... they're all looking backwards over each other's shoulder."

MIKE SMITH

"You just can't hypothesise about something that may or may not happen."

RODNEY MARSH

"The defender was so laid-back there he was almost vertical."

FRANK STAPLETON

"England is my home town."

MICHAEL OWEN

"Armstrong is about to join a list which includes only himself."

MARK BROWN

"Kleivert has back-heeled it through his own legs."

RODNEY MARSH

"Nicholas Jalabert does not have quite the same pedigree as his brother Jalabert."

MIKE SMITH

"One word to describe it would be absolutely pathetic!"

ALAN HANSEN

"Whatever anyone says about him [Wayne Rooney] is true."

ALAN SHEARER

"... a few bad results and they are staring down the barrel of the sack."

ANDY TOWNSEND

"Mido goes down clutching his right head."

ALAN GREEN

"I know what my strengths are, and I know what my not strengths are."

ADRIAN BOOTHROYD

"He's making all kinds of hand signals but no one can hear him."

JOHN MURRAY

"That's really one of those double-ended sticks..."

LAWRIE SANCHEZ

"You've hit the word right on the head."

RAY WILKINS

"... and he has lit the fuse to a match that was already boiling..."

ALAN PARRY

"If he opens his legs, he'll be hard to handle."

GRAHAM TAYLOR

"The barometer is still the bread and butter, especially away from home."

MIKE INGHAM

"Their problems have opened the door for a new face to step into their shoes."

'THE INSIDER'

"This is his first time back at the new stadium."

TOSH McKINLAY

"Disappointment would be way down my list of adjectives."

GORDON STRACHAN

"We don't set ourselves sights, but we know what we've got to aim for."

PAUL ROBINSON

"It's nice for us to have a fresh face in the camp sometimes for us to bounce things off..."

LAWRIE SANCHEZ

"They have now got the grit between their teeth."

KEVIN GALLAGHER

"One bad apple in the dressing room and everything can go pear-shaped."

PAUL MASEFIELD

"He's gone down like he's been felled by a tree."
ANDY GRAY

"They [Fulham] out-thought us mentally, and physically..."
STUART PEARCE

"Bolton's plan is to put Arsenal on the back foot in the air."
GARTH CROOKS

"They've got to be breaking that voodoo over Sweden."
LEE DIXON

"Bramble just threw his head at it."

TONY GUBBA

"... if you keep looking backwards in football, you'll fall flat on your face."

NICKY BUTT

"As soon as Lee Trundle scored that early goal for Swansea you always knew this wasn't going to be a nil-nil draw."

MATT JONES

"Paul Scholes is the most complete midfield player. He's got the lot. There's not a weakness he hasn't got."

STEVE BRUCE

"Sheringham's coming on. They broke the mint when they made this one."

BBC2

"If Livingston don't keep their discipline the inevitable could happen."

MARK HATELEY

"Crouch doesn't have the speed of quickness."

DAVID PLEAT

"In Manchester you are either Blue or Red... there's no two ways about it."

CHRIS COOPER

"France and Greece. Is this David versus Goliath and can Greece keep up their Cinderella form?"

COLLEEN JONES

"... well, it's a double-sided coin, John."

CHRIS KAMARA

"These tournaments only come around every two years, so you can't expect to win it every year."

MICHAEL OWEN

"Rangers await the arrival of Dado Prso – the only man in Scottish football with no vowels in his name."

JIM DELAHUNT

"Our central defenders, Doherty and Anthony Gardner, were fantastic and I told them that when they go to bed tonight they should think of each other."

DAVID PLEAT

"Martin O'Neill doesn't rush into the transfer market and when he does rush in he rushes in slowly."

JIM TRAYNOR

"The referee waved his head and said play on."

CONOR MacNAMARA

"Thornton... was the best man on the field by a long way, but the rest of the Rovers team weren't far behind him."

DONCASTER ROVERS WEBSITE

"Paulo Maldini – ageless. He's 39 this summer."

ITV

"If they [Greece] can beat Spain again, it will be a good scalpel."

IAN WRIGHT

"I can't say I wasn't sad not to see Steven Gerrard's name on the Liverpool team sheet."

BRYAN ROBSON

"They were swarming around him like a wet blanket."

GERRY ARMSTRONG

"The Liverpool fans would like to see Kewell back to the form he was in at Leeds, where he regularly roasted full backs."

SKY SPORTS

"There was no doubt about it, so the ref gave the defender the benefit of the doubt."

DAVE BASSETT

"Players have got to self-regulate each other."

MARTIN JOL

"And Hibs will just have to take that bodyblow on the chin."

CRAIG PATERSON

"Liverpool are banging their heads on a brick wall; they cannot find the door."

RADIO 5 LIVE

"With Messi going off they've lost one half of their magic box."

DAVID PLEAT

"Gallas's diving header was the last kick of the game."

JOHN INVERDALE

"That's a miss by his standards."

DAVID PLEAT

"When it comes to Michael Owen's foot, there will be a cut-off date when it's right or not."

MIKE PARRY

"His shot just rifled past the post slightly."

GRAEME LE SAUX

"Palace probably don't want to lose as much as they'd like to win."

CHRIS KAMARA

"It's come off his chest or his head or his shoulder, one of the two."

FRANK McCLINTOCK

"It looks like being a great second half – hold onto your seatbelts!"

PETER BRACKLEY

"At the beginning of the game there was only one team who could lose it, and sure enough only one team is losing."

KEVIN BLACKWELL

"What is always important, whether it's a win or a victory, is your next game."

GRAHAM TAYLOR

"For Burton, to play Man United in this replay is a one-off."

IAN WRIGHT

"The flag is being waved vociferously by the referee's assistant."

RADIO NEWCASTLE

"I didn't say them things I said."

GLENN HODDLE

"We kick ourselves in the foot all the time."

BBC RADIO OXFORD

"Rangers were two-nil up against Falkirk and took their foot off the handbrake."

RAY WILKINS

"What will he do? Exactly the same, but in a different way..."

BBC1

"He may have said it in Spanish but the referee is Italian and so he'll know what he said."

GRAEME LE SAUX

"To be fair on Senderos, he completely messes it up."

NIGEL WINTERBURN

"It was the perfect penalty – apart from he [Thierry Henry] missed it."

ROB McCAFFREY

"It was 0-0. So you could say we didn't score."

SIR ALEX FERGUSON

"You don't lose many games if you keep a clean sheet every week."

RADIO 5 LIVE

"At half-time we were 3-0 up and we had to be careful that they [Sheffield Wednesday] didn't get their legs between their tails in the second half."

CAMERON JEROME

"Our goalkeeper hasn't had a save to make but he still had to pick the ball out of the net four times."

JOE ROYAL

"Of course, they [Chelsea] have had all the money to spend. But, sometimes, that can be its own crutch to bear."

RADIO 5 LIVE

"The problem was in our heads – well, mentally."

STUART PEARCE

"This game was about the result."

STEVE BRUCE

"There's a few unknowns that we don't know about."

GLENN HODDLE

"British referees are every bit as good as their compatriots from other countries."

DAVID PLEAT

"Dyer had three options. He could have stood there with his hands by his side, but putting his hands down by his side wasn't an option. He could have run away, but running away wasn't an option. So he had to defend himself."

FREDDY SHEPHARD

"He was a good buy for us from Olympiakos on a free."

SAM ALLARDYCE

"Crewe started the weekend in 17th – the point moves them up a place to 18th."

GEORGE GAVIN

"He's got good clean feet."

GRAHAM TAYLOR

"They're dominating the possession when they have it, Chelsea."

ROBBIE EARLE

"You have to separate the facts from the reality, and the reality in this case is that there isn't one."

RADIO 3

"It just hasn't happened for them, for whatever reason, but they'll be hoping to build on that."
MICKY ADAMS

"He's gone in to countless challenges, and won both of them."
GUY MOWBRAY

"He [Lehmann] attacks his own mind internally..."
PAUL WALSH

"They [Liverpool] aren't playing at a high tempo, they're playing at a speed tempo."
TERRY VENABLES

"... banging the trumpet for the Anfield club..."
GEORGIE BINGHAM

"Liverpool have been more consistent in their last 12 games – five wins, three draws and four defeats."
SKY SPORTS

"Joe Cole passes to his namesake – Lampard."
JOHN MOTSON

"Martin O'Neill told us he's playing a 4-4-2 formation but he might be trying to pull the wool over the garden path."
DOUGIE DONNELLY

"It's football's equivalent of a yellow card."

GORDON TAYLOR

"Not wanting to harbour the point..."

MARK LAWRENSON

"To win international matches these days you've got to score."

IAN WALSH

"And Fulham are not retreating out of their shells much at all..."

RADIO 5 LIVE

"... all of this left the referee costing us more than what we should have got."

SAM ALLARDYCE

"David Beckham has been the victim of his own downfall."

RADIO FIVE LIVE

"... the player who stood out for me, who didn't even play, was Carrick."

LEE DIXON

"I was 24 and asked to sign for Rangers. Only a balloon would have said no."

STEVEN THOMPSON

"Whilst we get on and forget him [striker Sam Parkin], he will be forgotten with very fond memories."

ANDY KING

"Players like Thierry Henry are the icing on the cake but you need the mixture first. You need the dough, the bread and butter to hold it all together."

TONY ADAMS

Golf

"The door is now open for him [Tiger Woods] to really kick it in..."

JOHN INVERDALE

"And Vijay Singh lampoons another one down the fairway..."

KEN BROWN

"He [Tiger Woods] did it with the relentless bludgeoning of a master craftsman."

ANDREW COTTER

"And Tiger Woods picked up two birdies on the way home for a 69."

RADIO 4

Horse racing

"You must be lost for words – describe the feeling."

DEREK THOMPSON

"Horses have minds of their own, to a certain extent."

BBC

"The horse sadly died this morning, so it looks like he won't be running in the Gold Cup."

CHARLIE McCANN

"Paul [Makin] is a good guy; he puts his mouth where his face is."

DEREK THOMPSON

Literally

"The vehicles used in the raid were literally dangled under the noses of the Kent Constabulary."

CHANNEL 4 NEWS

"Muslims were literally glued to their televisions..."

RADIO 5 LIVE

"Bolton are literally encamped on the edge of the box."

LAWRIE SANCHEZ

"Poland have absolutely literally torn Azerbaijan to pieces."

PATRICK KINGHORN

"... literally hundreds of millions of poor countries in Africa..."

PETER HAIN

"Josh Lewsey has been literally cutting men in half all afternoon."

JASON LEONARD

"McSheffrey literally danced past three red shirts."

BERNIE SLAVEN

"Ricky Ponting is quite literally on fire."

MARK NICHOLAS

"... you can literally get away with murder twice a day on stage."

TOYAH WILLCOX

"He [batsman VVS Laxman] literally murdered Shane Warne on the last Australian tour."

L. SIVA RAMAKRISHNAN

"Schumacher literally killed the opposition yesterday."

ITV

"Once Southampton conceded a goal, they literally fell to pieces."

RADIO 5 LIVE

"Aston Villa literally didn't turn up for the game."

NIALL QUINN

"Literally, the ball was tied to his [George Best's] boots."

RICHARD PARK

"Liverpool came literally back from the grave."
ITV NEWS

"Are there moments when your heart is literally in your mouth?"
BBC1

Motor Sport

"Coulthard and Villeneuve are battling it out for last place."
MARTIN BRUNDLE

"The bandwagon had to fall off the rails."
BEN EDWARDS

"There's Montoya – you can see his mind working inside his head."

STEVE RIDER

"They [Ferarri] win together, they lose together, and no one else can beat them."

JAME ALLEN

"At the end of the day, it's a long day ahead of us."

NATASHA FIRMAN

Music

"You just have to oil the batteries every now and then."

LEO SAYER

"And [the conductor] there, really pulling the fat from the fire."

SIMON BATES

"Coldplay – they're one of the biggest-selling bands in the world, bar none."

BEN JONES

"The sun is getting longer and the days are getting shorter."

SIMON BATES

"It really lives up to its name, doesn't it? Mahler's 4th Symphony."

NICK BAILEY

Oddballs

"He [David Beckham] is just pretending I'm rubbish at interviewing – which is why he keeps giving me all these one-sybil answers."

VICTORIA BECKHAM

"My advice [to Faria Alam] would be to keep her head down and see how things develop..."
MAX CLIFFORD

"I wish my dear departed dad was here, because he was like a father figure to me."
CONTESTANT, WEAKEST LINK

"Mary Magdalene... was perhaps married to Jesus Christ and fathered a child with him."
NIGEL FLOYD

"The trouble with so many of them [budget airlines] is that they land 50 miles from the nearest airport."
MICKEY CLARK

"Up there in the audience is friend and fellow teacher Kelly, who's grinning like some sort of Cheshire cheese."

CHRIS TARRANT

"She may have her knockers but punters think Jordan will come out on top."

WARREN LUSH

"Gender has nothing to do with being a man or a woman."

NICKY CAMPBELL

"There are rumours that Caravaggio had a corpse dug up as a model for this picture of the dead Lazarus to make it as lifelike as possible."

TIM MARLOW

"Yes, the lance has been boiled."

SKY NEWS

"So there you are thinking you've died of something and you've died of something else."

SUSAN McREYNOLDS

"The problem is that the illnesses began to pile up, likc dominoes falling."

SKY NEWS

"This is the first time this plane has taken off from the ground."

BBC NEWS 24

"Once separated from the rest, the baboon's a sitting duck."

STEVE LEONARD

"I'll be back in just 15 minutes in an hour's time."

KIRSTY YOUNG

"They haven't got a bean to rub together."

FI GLOVER

"He's got a good brain on his shoulders."

PAUL DICKENSON

"I thought I should put my feet where my mouth is."

CARDINAL CORMACK MURPHY O'CONNOR

"Words can't say what I mean."

CHANTELLE

"The woman with the face transplant was in the papers today. I thought she would keep a lower profile."

ROGER DAY

"This global terrorism is everywhere..."

MADONNA

"When Mbayo gets back home at the end of the afternoon, she cooks and washes her children."

BBC NEWS

"The image of sperm donors as hard-up students short of cash is changing."

JANE DRAPER

"At the end of the day, you have got to have the balls to be feminine."

SUSANNAH CONSTANTINE

"I only speak French, I don't speak anything else."

KRISTIN SCOTT-THOMAS

"It's very difficult to walk a tightrope around these issues."

RADIO 4

"They've put their heads above the precipice."

MARGARET GILMORE

"We have knocked on thousands of doorsteps..."

MARY SCANLON

"It's a misconception that girls get themselves pregnant to get a council home."

RADIO 5 LIVE

"Professor Gearty is hanging his hat on a red herring."

RADIO 4

"Ivanuaskas' expression hasn't changed at all. He's just sitting there, polka-dot-faced."

ANDY GILLIES

"This will be the first time that people have won things single-handedly together."

CHANNEL 4

"In the Shoreditch case, they drew up a shortlist. It wasn't a very long shortlist..."

SARAH MONTAGUE

"It's a case of burglar turned gamekeeper."

CRAIG PATERSON

"The person that wins will be the one who sticks their neck out and pulls it off."

BBC2

"We found ourselves on a wild goose cul-de-sac."

RADIO 5 LIVE

"The River Thames, whilst always the same, is perpetually changing..."

ITV

"Even amongst his peers, he [Ronnie Barker] was peerless."

BBC1 NEWS

"This is Dizzy Gillespie, before his death, explaining how it all came together."

CHRISTIAN ROBINSON

"It is very hard to make predictions – particularly about the future."

PROFESSOR STEVE JONES

"This exhibition of work from Playboy... features some seminal moments in the magazine's history."

GEORGIE PALMER

"Homosexuality is causing painful splits in the Church of England."

BILL TURNBULL

"It's a chore watching cricket on TV. It's better to see it on the radio."

GRAHAM BEECROFT

"I've breast-fed myself and it's not easy."

JANE GARVEY

"The couple (Chris Flanagan and Henry Kane) who are amongst the first to get married under the new civil partnership legislation emerged from the Belfast registry office and happily flashed their rings to those who had gathered outside."

BBC NEWS

"The reason we've had to close our Home Furnishings store is because we were too contemporary, too soon."

ITN

"You look great for your age and I have no idea how old you are."

STEVE WRIGHT

"Alcoholism isn't an illness, it's a disease. Well, not a *disease*, more like an illness."

PAUL GASCOIGNE

"One area that we have failed to succeed in so far is toilets on trains. This continues to be a major weakness and a great frustration for passengers and staff alike. The good news is that I think we have now bottomed out what the real problems are..."

SOUTH-EASTERN TRAINS WEBSITE

"Nick Kochan has written a book about money laundering called 'The Washing Machine'. He is on the line now."

SARAH MONTAGUE

"Not only are they getting older, they're living longer."

TIM SMITH

"When she sees a sub-text, she has a tendency to grab at it like a drowning woman in a desert."

ALAN STRACHAN

"We don't need the hours and minutes nailed down."

JOHN TRICKETT

"When exactly does pink become light red? It's a grey area."

RADIO 5 LIVE

"I'd like to welcome a man who topped the best-seller list; in fact, he made number one."

PAUL O'GRADY

"He's very brainy; mentally as well as physically."

DEREK WHYTE

"Norwich [NHS Trust] have just appointed 14 Polish dentists to fill a gap."

BBC

"I don't have a crystal ball, and I haven't brought it with me tonight."

ED BALLS

"You can hear the raised eyebrows and the raspberries being blown."

ANDREW MARR

"Author J.K. Rowling today confirmed the name of the sixth book in the Harry Potter trilogy."

TOBY BENNETT

"Do you choose your own underwear or does your wife have a hand in it?"

HEATHER STOTT

"... Memorial carries the names of the unknown who fell in the war."

SKY NEWS

"So I understand you have had both legs amputated due to a long-standing medical problem."

JEREMY VINE

"When did you last see Skegness beach this deserted in July? Probably Christmas."

STEVE BRUCE

"Prediction's very difficult especially for the future."

PAUL LEWIS

"The Queen is 80 today. We'll be asking a deposed king – Constantine of Greece – what makes a successful monarch."

SHAUN LEY

"Isn't there a danger that you're crying wolf before the stable door has bolted?"

JON SNOW

"Many children attend school without a permanent head."

MIKE BAKER

"I look out for any slightest symptoms of bird flu in my family. I'm watching like a hawk."

NGUYEN THANH HUNG

"Now, if you are listening to this programme sitting in a traffic jam you are probably not alone."

GITTO HARRI

"I have just set up a foundation for less underprivilged children."

DICKIE BIRD

Olympicballs

"He's got so much potential and most of it is still to be realised."

STUART STOREY

"Diving will go onwards and upwards from here."

PETE WATERFIELD

"Coming last is not the best position."

SIR STEVE REDGRAVE

"And they're a bit short tonight, the Chinese."

BARRY DAVIES

"The marathon follows the famous historic route from the Battle of Marathon to the Panathinaikos Stadium."

BBC

"Ethiopia – the country who have won everything in distance running but they have never won the Marathon."

BRENDAN FOSTER

"From some areas on the steps, you can get a view of the Acropolis and there's not many sporting arenas around the world where you can say that."

ELEANOR OLDROYD

"His recovery from career-ending injuries is almost complete."

DAVID COLEMAN

"And the three of them are single-handedly pulling Australia apart."

BBC OLYMPIC HOCKEY

"And Obikwelu... walking round with his shoulders on his hips..."

JOHN RAWLING

"And Dick Palmer has been with the Olympic Games since he was almost born."

BBC NEWS

"I can't be dishappy with that."

ELIZABETH TWEEDLE

"She [Shelley Rudman] beat everybody to take silver in the Skeleton."

LORNA DUNKLEY

"Invariably the winner has won."

TERRY EDWARDS

"Gebreselassie was never able to do that – which was a shame because, at his best, he was capable of it."

STEVE CRAM

"It's ironic that this year a Greek athlete could or couldn't win the 200-metre sprint."

NICK MULLINS

"Of course, a great deal more people have silver medals than gold."

JOHN INVERDALE

"Greek weightlifting has certainly had its ups and downs."

STEVE RIDER

"And now, back to the Women's Beach Volleyball, where we have an all-Brazilian quarter-final for you..."

CLARE BALDING

"A young man [Mark Lewis-Francis] with so much potential – and most of it yet to be realised."

STUART STOREY

"... and I am delighted to say that Great Britain have just won their first gold medal. It will be hung around the necks of Shirley Robertson, Sarah Webb and Sarah Ayton."

CLAIRE MERCER

"There's three paddlers crossed the line in 2nd, 3rd, 4th and 5th."

BBC

"I put my cards on the bike and went pretty hard. When I got to the run I had spent all my biscuits, but that's the way it goes."

ANDREW JOHNS

"She has been a child prodigy since she was a youngster."

KARCH KIRALY

"You won't win silver medals at the Olympic Games unless you're the very very best."

BRENDAN FOSTER

"And Kelly is not one for hiding her heart on her sleeve."

DANNY WILLIAMS

Politics

"Even if he is executed and becomes a martyr to the Iraqis, I think Saddam can live with that."

CON COUGHLIN

"For too long the other main political parties have damaged Northern Ireland politics. It's our turn."

ALLIANCE PARTY SPOKESMAN

"It would be like chasing a dead duck around the farmyard..."

CHRIS PATTEN

"Tony Blair and Gordon Brown are caught between rival millstones."

JAMES COX

"If he [Birmingham Central Mosque chairman Dr Mohammed Naseem] wants to make cheap political points then he really ought to relinquish his position as chairman and let somebody who is neutral and has the interests of the community do it."

KHALID MAHMOOD

"There's a history to Iran, as there is to many other countries."

JACK STRAW

"I'll be surprised, I'll put it no stronger than that... I'll be very surprised indeed."

CHARLES KENNEDY

"Sinn Fein are the same sides of different coins."

BILL LOWRY

"The fact is that when a suicide bomber strikes once, he or she may strike again."

JOHN SIMPSON

"That has always been my position for a long time."

JOHN PRESCOTT

"I do not want to bang my own trumpet..."

SIR MALCOLM RIFKIND

"The idea of 24-hour drinking is not 24-hour drinking."

DAVID BLUNKETT

"If he [David Davis] wins, he will win with a cloud over his shoulder."

MATTHEW PARRIS

"The name Bin Laden means only one thing – terror. It also means fear."

PHILIP SCHOFIELD

"Leeds is the biggest city of its size in Europe."
GREG MULHOLLAND

"Democracy is a valley which flows in the veins of every citizen of the world."
JACK STRAW

"We will not be putting aircraft in the air that cannot fly."
MoD SPOKESMAN

"... if he [David Cameron] chooses this route, he'll find it a very, very hard road to plough."
MICHAEL PORTILLO

"I hope it will encourage people to speak out against what they believe in."
SHABINA BEGUM

"What worries me is the blanket description 'under 16s'. What about ten year-olds?"
ANNE WIDDECOMBE

"Obesity is a problem of considerable proportions."
MELANIE JOHNSON

Question & Answer

OLD MAN: I tried to commit suicide. I took 20 tablets and then called the doctor.

KIM RILEY: And you survived?

BBC LOOK EAST

INTERVIEWER: And so this is your first baby?

PROUD MUM: No, he's my third.

INTERVIEWER: Does he have any brothers or sisters?

RADIO 5 LIVE

TONY CASCARINO: How old are you?

CALLER: 40.

CASCARINO: Same as me – 41.

TALKSPORT RADIO

MARTIN TYLER: And what about Wayne Rooney?

ALAN SMITH: Brilliant. He never fails to disappoint.

SKY SPORTS

GARY RICHARDSON: What are the dangers of building Murray up?

GERALD WILLIAMS: First thing is it's inevitable. The second thing is, it's going to happen anyway...

RADIO 4

KEN BRUCE: And you're planning a gap year?

CALLER: Yes, from January.

KEN BRUCE: And you'll be away for how long?

CALLER: Er... around 12 months.

RADIO 2

Rugby

"One of the worst things you can do against a good side is beat them."

JOSH LEWSEY

"... it was the icing on the cake of disappointment."

JAMES SIMPSON-DANIEL

"It's just two young bulls testing their antelopes."

GARETH CHILCOTT

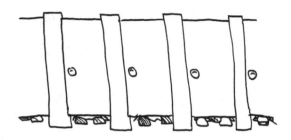

"They're a bit laxative."

ROBBIE PAUL

"I can't see into the future but he [Matthew Tait] is destined for great things."

ROBBIE PAUL

"It looks as if it had the legs, but just didn't have the distance."

SKY SPORTS

"People were looking around like headless chickens..."

DEWI MORRIS

"Australia have got their tails between their teeth at the moment."

NIGEL STARMER-SMITH

"Scotland are staring down the barrels of a wooden spoon."

MARTIN BAYFIELD

"This one's a bit easier because it's a lot more difficult."

JONATHAN DAVIES

Snooker

"It's easy to keep losing at this game. It's a lot harder to keep winning."

WILLIE THORNE

"At this level you pay for those prices."

STEVE DAVIS

"This isn't a rational decision – I've been thinking about this for quite a while."

RONNIE O'SULLIVAN

"China is like a different world... it's like a different country."

STEVE DAVIS

"It's not a matter of personality, it's the balls who are the enemy."

STEVE DAVIS

"There's a good twelve inches between the two red balls."

BBC

"'Throw caution to the wind'? It's a risky thing to do!"

JOHN VIRGO

"It's a lonely place out there in the middle of the table."

STEVE DAVIS

Swimming

"She's on the shoulder of the Hungarian swimmer who is two lanes away."

BOB BALLARD

Tennis

"And Federer becomes only the third player to achieve this impossible feat."

RADIO 5 LIVE

"He [Puerta] hit that shot with both feet off the air."

JOHN LLOYD

"Henman a winner as he loses again."
SIMON BARNES

"She [Sharapova] has got her head on her shoulders."
VIRGINIA WADE

"And there's Denton, his head hanging skywards..."
WIMBLEDON TENNIS COMMENTATOR

"The Australians and the French have a reciprocal arrangement to let young players get into each other's draws."
VIRGINIA WADE

"Tennis is a funny game; unbelievable highs and the lows are just as low..."

JOHN McENROE

"She's definitely improved a lot, even compared to when she was at her best."

KIM CLIJSTERS

"Tennis that's heads and tails above anything else we've seen."

TRACY AUSTIN

"But he [Federer] just keeps his feet churning."

JIMMY CONNORS

"You [Elena Baltacha] are the daughter of two famous sportsmen..."

RUSSELL FULLER

"Henman and Coria have met three times in the past and they've won one apiece."

ANNABEL CROFT

"Sharapova never got down on herself."

TRACY AUSTIN

World Cup Balls

"He's very quick for a man of his age. I suppose you'd call him ageless. He's 33 or 34."
DAVID PLEAT

"If we do win this one it won't be a bad thing."
GARETH SOUTHGATE

"It's quite possible that Brazil could win this match but you've also got to say that it's an equal chance that they lose. The same, though, can't be said for Ghana."
ALAN HANSEN

"A deflection – that's what changed the course of the ball."
JIM BEGLIN, ITV1

"That's their tactic here – don't get beaten."
MICK MCCARTHY

"There's a real international flavour to this World Cup."
JIMMY ARMFIELD

"... and Ukraine still have three fresh legs to bring on..."

RADIO 5 LIVE

"That's what I like about his [Torres'] movement – standing still..."

DAVID PLEAT

"... and Cristiano Ronaldo has hit the ball with every inch of his body weight!"

ALAN DARK

"You need at least eight or nine men in a ten-man wall."

MARK LAWRENSON

"He knows all about the Italian opposition, playing now in Turkey..."

JOHN MOTSON

"Peter Crouch is absolutely centrifugal to England's World Cup chances."

MIKE PARRY

"Mexico are bringing on two new players so presumably they will be taking two off."

ITV

"It was really difficult for us playing in the midday sun with that three o'clock kick-off."

DAVID BECKHAM

"For a little player he's not very tall."

LIAM BRADY

"They [England] might do a Greece. Like Greece did."

TERRY BUTCHER

"The home crowd are worth half a goal to them."

LEE DIXON

"We wanted to nullify Ecuador and win the game and we achieved all three."

STEVE MCLAREN

"Beckham has one of the best passes in the game – providing there's another player at the end of it."

ITV

BBC REPORTER: Ten minutes before the game you did not know you were playing. When did you find out you were?

SHAKA HISLOP: Ten minutes before the game.

"Heavy defeat can sometimes work against you."

RADIO 5 LIVE

"The French and Italian flags are identical – apart from the colours."

RODNEY MARSH

"I'd love Wayne Rooney to be our next Zinedine Zidane because we've never had one before."

JASON CUNDY